# A·SHROPSHIRE·LAD
## BY·A.E.HOUSMAN

# A · SHROPSHIRE · LAD
## BY·A.E. HOUSMAN

### WOOD·ENGRAVINGS
### AGNES·MILLER·PARKER
### WITH·AN·INTRODUCTION
### BY·IAN·ROGERSON

TRAFALGAR·SQVARE
PUBLISHING

First published in the United States of America in 1996 by
Trafalgar Square Publishing, North Pomfret, Vermont 05053

**Printed in Great Britain by St Edmundsbury Press,
Bury St Edmunds, Suffolk**

ISBN 1 57076 058 6

Typeset by GW Typesetting, Willingham, Cambridge

# INTRODUCTION

## BY IAN ROGERSON

THIS introduction is not the place for an exercise in literary criticism. During the last half-century, hundreds of writers have focused upon Alfred Edward Housman: the influences upon him, his influence on others, his place in the pantheon of classical scholars and, of course, on his verse. In this respect, the major preoccupation of his critics is whether or not he is something more than a minor poet. One suspects that the very title, let alone the enduring popularity of *A Shropshire Lad*, has been an irritant to some scholars. It is unlikely that Housman, who spent the greater part of his life in an academic environment, had much sympathy with that industry known as English literary criticism, and it is quite likely that he gained a certain amount of innocent pleasure from scattering odd clues and the occasional misleading statement concerning the origin of these poems.

Not untypical of the controversy which surrounded *A Shropshire Lad* was the attack on Housman in the *New Statesman and Nation* where, after noting the obituaries which referred to him as a fine lyric poet, Cyril Connolly wrote a totally damning criticism of his verse, typified by such comments as "The fate which Housman's poems deserve, of course, is to be set to music by English composers and sung by English singers". Housman's bibliographer, the Oxford scholar John Sparrow, immediately responded by accusing Connolly of having "the satisfaction of arriving in time to spit on the grave before the mourners had departed". Connolly, however, had the last word. "I did not know that in the Sacred Wood of English Literature the poetry of Housman was a ju-ju tree, to touch which is punishable with torture or death."[1]

[9]

Housman was born at Fockbury, near Bromsgrove, Worcestershire, on 26th March 1859, the eldest of a large family which included a brother, Laurence, and a sister, Clemence, both of whom were to study wood engraving as a means of illustration. Laurence, who lived to a great age, was first an illustrator and latterly a writer. Remembered in literary circles for his plays on the domestic life of Queen Victoria, he also published a personal memoir on his more famous brother.[2] Christina Rossetti's poem *Goblin Market*, with Laurence's drawings engraved on the wood by Clemence, is regarded as one of the outstanding examples of nineteenth-century book design. Clemence, in addition to becoming a highly regarded wood engraver, also wrote, and her novel *Werewolf* first appeared as a serial in *Atalanta* and later in book form from John Lane, the most progressive English publisher of the 'nineties.

Early success eluded Alfred who, despite winning a scholarship to St John's College, Oxford, and showing signs of great learning, failed his examinations because his interests and deep knowledge of certain specialisms did not equate with the requirements of the examiners. As Professor Norman Page has pointed out, quoting Walter Raleigh, he was a victim of a system "where the nightingale got no prize at the poultry show".[3] Subsequently, he revisited Oxford to take the examinations for a pass degree but waited for ten years before he went through the formality of having it conferred.

Turning away from the prospect of an academic life, he took up a clerkship in the Patent Office. In his spare time, he continued to build up his knowledge of classical studies and succeeded in having some twenty-five scholarly papers published over a ten-year period. This brought him the recognition which he needed to obtain the Chair of Latin at University College London, the appointing committee having the good sense to recognise that his earlier failure was not due to a lack of scholarship, but rather an excess of that pursuit.

His inaugural lecture, delivered in 1892, was made widely available after his death and, along with John Henry Newman and Matthew Arnold, his views on culture and the idea of a university have been significant in that debate. Housman's contribution to raising standards at University College London, together with his proven capability for administration, have been amply recorded.[4] In 1911 he was offered the Chair of Latin at Cambridge, where he was to spend the rest of his life. It is, however, through a slim volume of verse and not through his considerable academic distinctions that his name has become familiar to generations of readers.

*A Shropshire Lad* is a collection of verse which is readily accessible, even to those who profess a distaste for poetry. Housman, in reply to a correspondent, indicated that he did not begin to write poetry in earnest until the really emotional part of his life was over. Housman's suppressed homosexuality, his unrequited sole love, the trial and subsequent imprisonment of Oscar Wilde are just a few examples of the factors considered to be the springs from which the verse emanated. Whilst Housman preferred his readers to believe that the bulk of the verse was written in the first half of 1895, it is possible that the writing could have begun earlier. What is certain is that the volume was offered first to Macmillan and Co, who rejected it. In 1896 it was first published by Kegan Paul in an edition of five hundred copies with a substantial financial contribution from the author. Vanity publishing was as common at that time as it is today and it is perhaps unsurprising that Kegan Paul fails to mention *A Shropshire Lad* in his memoirs. The sales of that first edition were slow and, when Grant Richards showed interest in taking over the title, Housman was not so much worried about the lack of sales but at the possibility of hurting Kegan Paul's feelings, a totally needless concern, as it turned out.

Whilst the bibliographical history of *A Shropshire Lad* is a happy hunting ground for those interested in minutiae, the important facts are beyond dispute. It was Alfred Pollard, a close friend, who first encouraged Housman to put his words into print and, when the author chose the title *Poems by Terence Hearsay*, persuaded him to publish under his own name.[5] When the second edition was published by Grant Richards, Housman stipulated that the author's share of the profits, if any, was to be put to reducing the price of further issues. It was not until 1922 that Housman decided to accept royalties on the title.[6]

At the turn of the century, Grant Richards was a young publisher with little sense of book design and whose enthusiasm for literature far outweighed his business acumen. Richards, in contrast to Kegan Paul, devoted a chapter of his autobiography to *A Shropshire Lad*, explaining that, on first approaching the author with a view to republishing the verse, he was rebuffed on the grounds that the first edition had not sold out. However, in due course the volume came to him and both author and publisher apparently enjoyed a pleasant relationship, despite Housman's irritability with Richards' failure to prevent typographical errors creeping into the successive printings. The title was not copyrighted in the United States of America and this led to pirated and unauthorised editions. The more ethically minded publishers who sent cheques across the Atlantic were no doubt surprised when these were returned, actions which many would consider highly unusual, but not to a poet who sent a considerable portion of his savings to the Chancellor of the Exchequer to aid the war effort. At one time, *A Shropshire Lad* enjoyed a greater popularity in the United States than in Britain. Richards believed that this was due to the publication of some of the verse in *MacClure's Magazine,* which then had an enormous circulation.[7]

The precarious publishing career of Grant Richards involved two bankruptcies and eventually his list was taken over by the Garnstone Press.[8] As late as 1994, poor reprints of early editions could still be found in public libraries, although the well-produced *Collected Poems of A. E. Housman*, first published by Jonathan Cape in 1939, has been widely available and infinitely more readable. Housman, who is on record as demanding legible type, had no idea of what constituted readability, that is the matching of typeface, type size, choice of paper and the design of the page to the nature of the literature in order to ensure the maximum comfort for the reader. Grant Richards, who should have known better, utterly failed the author in this respect. Despite Richards' lapses, an enduring friendship developed between publisher and author. One unforeseen outcome of the popularity of *A Shropshire Lad*, noted by the critic Stephen Williams, was the interest of Gurney, Butterworth, Ireland, Vaughan Williams and other contemporary composers who sought permissions from Richards and Housman and, by their musical settings of the lyrics, "helped themselves to fame and popularity".[9]

Richards was pleased with an illustrated edition which he published in 1908 with colour plates of Shropshire landscapes from paintings by William Hyde. At the time, Housman did not appear to be moved much one way or the other by this embellishment of his verse, but in a letter to Seymour Adelman written twenty years later he contemptuously referred to colour plates as vulgar, Hyde's presumably being no exception.[10] Adelman, a noted devotee of the work of Claud Lovat Fraser, must have been mortified to be told that "the late Lovat Fraser made drawings which he called illustrations...but illustrations they were not". In 1920, when Richards was working on a projected edition of *A Shropshire Lad* to be decorated by Fraser, Housman informed the flabbergasted publisher that "I should look a fool if I allowed the book to appear with these decorations". Fraser had dressed some of the characters in period costume and "to transpose into the 18th century a book which begins with Queen Victoria's Jubilee is the act of a rhinoceros".[11] However, admirers of Fraser's work thought sufficiently of the drawings to publish them in a limited edition as a picture book.[12] In this format, the spirited reed-pen drawings seem bereft of meaning.

Many of those writing on Housman convey a picture of a difficult and often intolerant bachelor. Housman's strongly expressed convictions on illustrators are not untypical of many of the comments to be found in his letters which reinforce this view. However, there were those close to him who saw another side to his nature. Percy Withers, who went up to Cambridge in 1917, remembers his kindness and, in particular, the "healing" letter promptly despatched to John Drinkwater who had been accused in *The Times* of plagiarising *A Shropshire Lad*, despite the fact that, privately, Housman had a poor view of Drinkwater as a poet.[13] A S Gow, who knew Housman well, wrote of *The Family*, a Cambridge dining club at which Housman "would pour out from his accurate and retentive memory anecdote and reminiscence with a felicity and economy of language which made him an admirable raconteur".[14]

It is unlikely that, if Housman had still been alive in 1940, he would have considered any proposal, however reasonable, for another illustrated edition, but Laurence Housman, his literary executor, obviously had no such reservations for in that year George

Harrap published an edition illustrated with wood engravings cut for the purpose by Agnes Miller Parker. Whilst that edition was no masterpiece of design, it was far more elegant a production than any that had gone before.

It is impossible to conjecture what Housman would have thought of Parker's art, but it is difficult to see that he could have argued that her wood engravings detracted from the text. By this time, she was at the height of her powers and her reputation as an illustrator was unsullied. Parker was no mere representational illustrator but a sensitive interpretative artist whose engravings invariably gave an added dimension to the text. That she succeeded with *A Shropshire Lad* is shown, at least in commercial terms, in that sufficient numbers of buyers were attracted to see the edition through thirteen impressions between 1940 and 1981.[15]

### THE ILLUSTRATOR

Agnes Miller Parker had come to prominence through her wood engraving for two of the finest private press books of the inter-war years. In 1930 her husband, the Scottish artist William McCance, had been appointed Controller of the Gregynog Press. In October of that year they took up residence at Tregaryn, near the great house at Newtown, Montgomeryshire, to work alongside Blair Hughes-Stanton and his wife Gertrude Hermes. This was a profoundly frustrating experience for the four artists due to the constant interruptions of the Misses Davies, the wealthy, Calvinistic and indecisive proprietors.[16] In those circumstances, it is scarcely possible to believe that the McCances could produce *The Fables of Esope* and *Twenty-One Welsh Gypsy Folk Tales*, major landmarks in the Private Press movement. Despite their difficulties they were more fortunate than the talented Gertrude Hermes, whose six wood engravings for Gilbert White's *The Natural History of Selborne* had to wait until the revived Gwasg Gregynog published them in 1988.

Whilst still at Tregaryn, Agnes was offered work by Robert Gibbings and, having no more employment in hand for Gregynog, proceeded to cut blocks for *Daisy Matthews*, by Rhys Davies and *The House with the Apricot*, by H E Bates. These were published by the

Golden Cockerel Press in limited editions in 1932 and 1933 respectively. The latter title was the probable inspiration for a major publishing initiative which was to make her famous in the world of books.

Parker's wood engravings for the Gregynog Press were a tour-de-force and established her reputation in the United States where there was a considerable interest in fine printing and illustration. Although at that time wood-engraved illustration was rarely employed in commercial book production, the publisher Victor Gollancz saw the possibilities of a successful combination of the countryside writings of H E Bates with the highly individual and flamboyant examples of decorative art which Agnes Miller Parker could bring to the page.

Gollancz understood good book design and was a master of publicity. These factors, together with striking dustwrappers and a feast of wood-engraved natural history illustration of the highest order to embellish Bates's lucid prose, ensured the success of *Through the Woods*, which was published in 1936. *Down the River*, published in the following year, was equally popular, and these titles, which were reprinted, brought her art and that of H E Bates before a wider public.

Bates obviously enjoyed the experience of working with the artist. Of her striking figure of the appalling gamekeeper in *Through the Woods*, he exclaimed "very good - just like him, my work is not up to the standard of your pictures".[17] Eight surviving pencil drawings of the gamekeeper, in varying poses, together with a large number of detailed plant drawings, demonstrate her meticulous preparation for these books, which contained seventy-three and eighty-three wood engravings respectively. Of the many wood engravers at work during the nineteen-thirties, only Clare Leighton's *Four Hedges* and *Country Matters,* also published by Gollancz, achieved similar popularity. Whilst the Gollancz books enhanced Parker's growing reputation and helped relieve her financial difficulties, she was anxious for more work. Book illustration was not highly paid and the cutting of a block was a slow process compared with the use of pen and ink.

Fortunately, her work had come to the attention of George Macy, owner of the Limited Editions Club of New York. Macy's high-class book club provided fine editions of the classics for a guaranteed readership of fifteen hundred subscribers. At this time he was pursuing a policy, as far as was possible, of having books designed and printed in the country of origin of the text. Agnes was contracted to produce thirty-two full-page engravings and a title-page vignette for an edition of Thomas Gray's *Elegy written in a Country Churchyard* to be published in 1938.

The illustration of Gray's verse was a new departure for Agnes and, for many of the illustrations, she employed the device of using the literal and the imaginative in the same picture. For example, a rural setting of reaper with scythe is bordered by cameos of a battle-scene and a royal throne. These stylistic images are not among the most popular of Parker's wood engravings, perhaps puzzling to readers more familiar with representational rather than interpretative illustration. It is unlikely that these illustrations would have been acceptable to a conventional publisher, but Macy was able to maximise his profits by first issuing the title in the Limited Editions Club and then reprinting the book from electros for his more down-market enterprise, the Heritage Press book club. The style which Agnes created for *Gray's Elegy* was to play an important part in her illustrations for *A Shropshire Lad*.

Macy also embarked upon a huge project to publish the works of William Shakespeare, designed by Bruce Rogers, with each play illustrated by a different artist. Agnes provided six very large and spectacular wood engravings for *Richard II*. After working on such a scale, she found it difficult to return to working on small individual blocks, the first of which was for a bookplate for a friend and patron, Philip Gibbons, with whom she corresponded for over forty years. She then moved immediately on to the designs for *A Shropshire Lad*, for Harrap's letter had come out of the blue at a time when she had no further commissions and the prospect of war was increasing day by day.

Highly descriptive, direct writing poses special problems for illustrators. Richard Le Gallienne, in reviewing *A Shropshire Lad* in *The Star* of 11 May 1896, unconsciously emphasised this point by describing the verse as "poems combining to paint a picture". When Agnes finished cutting the blocks for *A Shropshire Lad* in July 1940, it was with a sense of relief. She admitted to enjoying the work "despite the war and its horrors...and gave me no peace".[18] Including the title-page decoration, there were fifty-six illustrations to be drawn and engraved. This was a considerable undertaking, considering the relatively small amount of text involved.

Cleverly, she set the scene with a calm title-page vignette where the poet contemplates his landscape. Immediately following, there is a powerful tailpiece of a burning beacon, this image of the night sky being the forerunner to the similar scenes in her illustration of Hardy's *The Return of the Native*. The tailpiece to *Loveliest of trees, the Cherry now* is a modest cut, for no illustration could add much to twelve of the most poignant lines in the English language. However, Agnes had no such inhibitions about *The Recruit*, the first of the military pictures in the book where her exquisite, crisp tool work reveals a self-consciously smart soldier set against a background of Ludlow town.

The graveyard, a constant presence in the engravings for *Gray's Elegy*, is present in no less than seven poems in *A Shropshire Lad*, unsurprising when the verse is strewn with constant reminders of man's mortality. More significantly, however, there are examples of the composite pictures which first appeared in the Limited Editions Club title. Here, these enigmatic images are less successful than in the earlier book, being uneasy interjections between the solid, comfortable and pleasing images of townscape and countryside.

Francis Meynell was one of a number of perceptive typographers and book designers who have written on the difficulties in setting verse. Himself a poet, he drew attention to the fact that poetry needs to be read slowly and that readableness here was more important than legibility. Harrap's edition of *A Shropshire Lad* was set in Eric Gill's Perpetua, perhaps not the most appropriate typeface for the purpose, and there is a lack of uniformity in the setting of the poems. Some have all lines commencing at the margin, others have alternate lines inset. In some instances speech is printed in italics, and elsewhere not so. The inclusion of illustrations in poetry can cause further difficulties for the reader, but in this edition damage was minimised by restricting the use of the wood engravings primarily to head- and tailpieces.

As could be expected, Agnes hoped for favourable reviews of her work and was concerned by a lack of critical comment, complaining that she had not seen a single review of Harrap's edition. R A Maynard, one-time Controller of the Gregynog Press and printer of *Gray's Elegy*, told Agnes that it was a rotten book from a typographical point of view, at which she wanted "to bury myself in one of the nearby (bomb) craters".[19] The insufficiencies of design could hardly be blamed on the war which, at that time, had scarcely begun to affect those printers with large stocks of good-quality paper. In the hard winter of 1941, she wrote to Gibbons of "her love of the heavy skies, the dark, lacy bare trees, the white snow with clean cut and dark forms of animals and birds, like Breughel's landscapes", imagery in fact of her own expressive art.[20] Shrugging off her disappointment, she was soon immersed in her work on *The Return of the Native*. This was the first of the five major novels of Thomas Hardy which Agnes was to illustrate for Macy's book clubs. Embarking on this project, she expressed her reservations to Gibbons because she felt that "Hardy describes so well that illustrators to me seem superfluous... is it that the ordinary reader does not form visual pictures?".[21]

The experiences of interpreting Thomas Gray and A E Housman no doubt overcame any reservations she had about attempting Hardy or responding to an invitation from the Lutterworth Press to illustrate some essays of Richard Jefferies, another highly descriptive nature writer. This project eventually grew to five volumes, each sensitively edited by Samuel J Looker and demanding twenty-four wood engravings. *The Spring of the Year*, *The Life of the Fields*, *Field and Hedgerow*, *The Old House at Coate* and *The Open Air* appeared between 1946 and 1948, when war economy standards were still in force. In letters to Gibbons, Agnes expressed her disappointment and apologised for their "schoolbook look". Despite her reservations, there is much to admire in these pocket-sized volumes, which today are eagerly sought after. Her ingenuity in achieving variety and interest whilst working within permitted dimensions is apparent. A suggestion from the publishers that she should illustrate further volumes of Jefferies' essays was rejected as she felt that "five Jefferies books is enough". Her heartfelt wish to illustrate Gilbert White's *The Natural History of Selborne* "when we can get really good paper and pre-war conditions" did not materialise.[22] An opportunity was missed, for Lutterworth Press used the line drawings of John Nash for their edition of 1951.

To rub salt into the wound, Nash was given a further opportunity to illustrate *Selborne* for the Limited Editions Club's edition of 1972. Many others have tried their hand at embellishing the detailed descriptive writings of Gilbert White, with varying degrees of success. It is a matter of regret that Agnes Miller Parker did not have that chance for, in retrospect, it would seem that such a project, sensitively handled by the right publisher, could have produced one of the great illustrated books of the twentieth century.

Her clear vision, combined with an astonishing virtuosity of technique, was responsible for an array of black and white illustration which, in its genre, is unrivalled. Clare Leighton, her contemporary during the nineteen-thirties, described her as "one of the most highly skilled engravers living. No one can equal her in her delicate merging of blacks into whites through infinite varyings of greys".[23] George Macy, writing to his subscribing members, was in no doubt as to who was the finest twentieth-century wood engraver. "It may not be true that Mrs McCance is the finest wood-engraver in the world to-day, but there are dozens of competent authorities who say she is."[24]

The art of wood engraving is to release light from the block. Agnes Miller Parker's skill with the burin was of such an order that her blocks, when printed, positively radiate light. She could infuse the most mundane subject with sparkle and, at times, achieved such a level of coruscation in her illustration that verbal description becomes virtually meaningless. The wood engravings for *A Shropshire Lad* may rank among her minor works but she gave them equal love and attention. It is a pity that Housman was not alive when these were executed. As a professional himself, he would have found much to admire.

## REFERENCES

1. Connolly, C. A E Housman: a Controversy, reprinted in *The Condemned Playground: Essays 1927-1944*. London, Routledge, 1945, pp47-62.

2. Housman, L. *A E H: Some Poems, Some Letters and a Personal Memoir*. London, Cape, 1937.

3. Page, N. *A E Housman: A Critical Biography*. London, Macmillan, 1983, p16.

4. Graves, R P. *A E Housman, the Scholar Poet*. London, Routledge and Kegan Paul, 1979.

5. Page, N. op cit, p85.

6. Maas, H. ed. *The Letters of A E Housman*. London, Hart-Davis, 1971, p49.

7. Richards, G. *Author Hunting: Memories of Years Mainly Spent in Publishing*. New ed. London, Unicorn Press, 1960, p87.

8. Carter, J and Sparrow, J. *A E Housman: A Bibliography*. 2nd ed. Winchester, St Paul's Bibliographies, 1982, p8.

9. Richards, G. *Housman, 1897-1936*. London, Oxford University Press, 1941, p87.

10. Maas, H. op cit, pp96, 265.

11. Maas, H. op cit, pp181, 265.

12. *Sixty-Three Unpublished Designs. Claud Lovat Fraser*. London, The First Editions Club, 1924.

13. Withers, P. *A Buried Life: Personal Recollections of A E Housman*. London, Cape, 1940, p42.

14. Gow, A S. *A E Housman: A Sketch*. Cambridge, Cambridge University Press, 1936, p50.

15. Carter, J. and Sparrow. op cit, p8.

16. Harrop, D. *A History of the Gregynog Press*. London, Private Libraries Association, 1980, pp90 et seq.

17. Bates, H E. Letter to Agnes Miller Parker dated 19 Aug 1936. National Library of Scotland. AMP archive box no 326.

18. Parker, A M. Letter to Philip Gibbons dated 1 Oct 1940. Victoria and Albert Museum. National Art Library. Box MS L26 1983.

19. Parker, A M. Letter to Philip Gibbons dated 3 Dec 1940. V & A Coll.

20. Parker, A M. Letter to Philip Gibbons dated 19 Jan 1942. V & A Coll.

21. Parker, A M. Letter to Philip Gibbons dated 21 Feb 1941. V & A Coll.

22. Parker, A M. Letter to Philip Gibbons dated 15 Jun 1948. V & A Coll.

23. Leighton, C. *Wood Engraving and Woodcuts*. New ed. London, Studio Publications, 1944.

24. Macy, G. Monthly Letter No 269. New York, Limited Editions Club, Dec 1955, p4.

## 1887

From Clee to heaven the beacon burns,
    The shires have seen it plain,
From north and south the sign returns
    And beacons burn again.

Look left, look right, the hills are bright,
    The dales are light between,
Because 'tis fifty years to-night
    That God has saved the Queen.

Now, when the flame they watch not towers
    About the soil they trod,
Lads, we'll remember friends of ours
    Who shared the work with God.

To skies that knit their heartstrings right,
    To fields that bred them brave,
The saviours come not home to-night:
    Themselves they could not save.

It dawns in Asia, tombstones show
    And Shropshire names are read;
And the Nile spills his overflow
    Beside the Severn's dead.

We pledge in peace by farm and town
    The Queen they served in war,
And fire the beacons up and down
    The land they perished for.

'God save the Queen' we living sing,
  From height to height 'tis heard;
And with the rest your voices ring,
  Lads of the Fifty-third.

Oh, God will save her, fear you not:
  Be you the men you've been,
Get you the sons your fathers got,
  And God will save the Queen.

Loveliest of trees, the cherry now
Is hung with bloom along the bough,
And stands about the woodland ride
Wearing white for Eastertide.

Now, of my threescore years and ten,
Twenty will not come again,
And take from seventy springs a score,
It only leaves me fifty more.

And since to look at things in bloom
Fifty springs are little room,
About the woodlands I will go
To see the cherry hung with snow.

## THE RECRUIT

Leave your home behind, lad,
    And reach your friends your hand,
And go, and luck go with you
    While Ludlow tower shall stand.

Oh, come you home of Sunday
    When Ludlow streets are still
And Ludlow bells are calling
    To farm and lane and mill,

Or come you home of Monday
    When Ludlow market hums
And Ludlow chimes are playing
    'The conquering hero comes,'

Come you home a hero,
    Or come not home at all,
The lads you leave will mind you
    Till Ludlow tower shall fall.

And you will list the bugle
    That blows in lands of morn,
And make the foes of England
    Be sorry you were born.

And you till trump of doomsday
    On lands of morn may lie,
And make the hearts of comrades
    Be heavy where you die.

Leave your home behind you,
　　Your friends by field and town:
Oh, town and field will mind you
　　Till Ludlow tower is down.

## REVEILLE

Wake: the silver dusk returning
  Up the beach of darkness brims,
And the ship of sunrise burning
  Strands upon the eastern rims.

Wake: the vaulted shadow shatters,
  Trampled to the floor it spanned,
And the tent of night in tatters
  Straws the sky-pavilioned land.

Up, lad, up, 'tis late for lying:
  Hear the drums of morning play;
Hark, the empty highways crying
  'Who'll beyond the hills away?'

Towns and countries woo together,
  Forelands beacon, belfries call;
Never lad that trod on leather
  Lived to feast his heart with all.

Up, lad: thews that lie and cumber
  Sunlit pallets never thrive;
Morns abed and daylight slumber
  Were not meant for man alive.

Clay lies still, but blood's a rover;
  Breath's a ware that will not keep.
Up, lad: when the journey's over
  There'll be time enough to sleep.

Oh see how thick the goldcup flowers
   Are lying in field and lane,
With dandelions to tell the hours
   That never are told again.
Oh may I squire you round the meads
   And pick you posies gay?
– 'Twill do no harm to take my arm.
   'You may, young man, you may.'

Ah, spring was sent for lass and lad,
   'Tis now the blood runs gold,
And man and maid had best be glad
   Before the world is old.
What flowers to-day may flower to-morrow,
   But never as good as new.
– Suppose I wound my arm right round –
   ''Tis true, young man, 'tis true.'

Some lads there are, 'tis shame to say,
   That only court to thieve,
And once they bear the bloom away
   'Tis little enough they leave.
Then keep your heart for men like me
   And safe from trustless chaps.
My love is true and all for you.
   'Perhaps, young man, perhaps.'

Oh, look in my eyes then, can you doubt?
    – Why, 'tis a mile from town.
How green the grass is all about!
    We might as well sit down.
– Ah, life, what is it but a flower?
    Why must true lovers sigh?
Be kind, have pity, my own, my pretty, –
    'Good-bye, young man, good-bye.'

When the lad for longing sighs,
　Mute and dull of cheer and pale,
If at death's own door he lies,
　Maiden, you can heal his ail.

Lovers' ills are all to buy:
　The wan look, the hollow tone,
The hung head, the sunken eye,
　You can have them for your own.

Buy them, buy them: eve and morn
　Lovers' ills are all to sell.
Then you can lie down forlorn;
　But the lover will be well.

When smoke stood up from Ludlow,
   And mist blew off from Teme,
And blithe afield to ploughing
   Against the morning beam
   I strode beside my team,

The blackbird in the coppice
   Looked out to see me stride,
And hearkened as I whistled
   The trampling team beside,
   And fluted and replied:

'Lie down, lie down, young yeoman;
   What use to rise and rise?
Rise man a thousand mornings
   Yet down at last he lies,
   And then the man is wise.'

I heard the tune he sang me,
   And spied his yellow bill;
I picked a stone and aimed it
   And threw it with a will:
   Then the bird was still.

Then my soul within me
   Took up the blackbird's strain,
And still beside the horses
   Along the dewy lane
   It sang the song again:

'Lie down, lie down, young yeoman;
    The sun moves always west;
The road one treads to labour
    Will lead one home to rest,
    And that will be the best.'

'Farewell to barn and stack and tree,
　　Farewell to Severn shore.
Terence, look your last at me,
　　For I come home no more.

'The sun burns on the half-mown hill,
　　By now the blood is dried;
And Maurice amongst the hay lies still
　　And my knife is in his side.

'My mother thinks us long away;
　　'Tis time the field were mown.
She had two sons at rising day,
　　To-night she'll be alone.

'And here's a bloody hand to shake,
　　And oh, man, here's good-bye;
We'll sweat no more on scythe and rake,
　　My bloody hands and I.

'I wish you strength to bring you pride,
　　And a love to keep you clean,
And I wish you luck, come Lammastide,
　　At racing on the green.

'Long for me the rick will wait,
　　And long will wait the fold,
And long will stand the empty plate,
　　And dinner will be cold.'

On moonlit heath and lonesome bank
   The sheep beside me graze;
And yon the gallows used to clank
   Fast by the four cross ways.

A careless shepherd once would keep
   The flocks by moonlight there,'
And high amongst the glimmering sheep
   The dead man stood on air.

They hang us now in Shrewsbury jail:
   The whistles blow forlorn,
And trains all night groan on the rail
   To men that die at morn.

There sleeps in Shrewsbury jail to-night,
   Or wakes, as may betide,
A better lad, if things went right,
   Than most that sleep outside.

And naked to the hangman's noose
   The morning clocks will ring
A neck God made for other use
   Than strangling in a string.

And sharp the link of life will snap,
   And dead on air will stand
Heels that held up as straight a chap
   As treads upon the land.

' Hanging in chains was called keeping sheep by moonlight.

So here I'll watch the night and wait
  To see the morning shine,
When he will hear the stroke of eight
  And not the stroke of nine;

And wish my friend as sound a sleep
  As lads' I did not know,
That shepherded the moonlit sheep
  A hundred years ago.

## MARCH

The Sun at noon to higher air,
Unharnessing the silver Pair
That late before his chariot swam,
Rides on the gold wool of the Ram.

So braver notes the storm-cock sings
To start the rusted wheel of things,
And brutes in field and brutes in pen
Leap that the world goes round again.

The boys are up the woods with day
To fetch the daffodils away,
And home at noonday from the hills
They bring no dearth of daffodils.

Afield for palms the girls repair,
And sure enough the palms are there,
And each will find by hedge or pond
Her waving silver-tufted wand.

In farm and field through all the shire
The eye beholds the heart's desire;
Ah, let not only mine be vain,
For lovers should be loved again.

On your midnight pallet lying,
    Listen, and undo the door:
Lads that waste the light in sighing
    In the dark should sigh no more;
Night should ease a lover's sorrow;
Therefore, since I go to-morrow,
    Pity me before.

In the land to which I travel,
    The far dwelling, let me say –
Once, if here the couch is gravel,
    In a kinder bed I lay,
And the breast the darnel smothers
Rested once upon another's
    When it was not clay.

When I watch the living meet,
   And the moving pageant file
Warm and breathing through the street
   Where I lodge a little while,

If the heats of hate and lust
   In the house of flesh are strong,
Let me mind the house of dust
   Where my sojourn shall be long.

In the nation that is not
   Nothing stands that stood before;
There revenges are forgot,
   And the hater hates no more;

Lovers lying two and two
   Ask not whom they sleep beside,
And the bridegroom all night through
   Never turns him to the bride.

When I was one-and-twenty
   I heard a wise man say,
'Give crowns and pounds and guineas
   But not your heart away;
Give pearls away and rubies
   But keep your fancy free.'
But I was one-and-twenty,
   No use to talk to me.

When I was one-and-twenty
   I heard him say again,
'The heart out of the bosom
   Was never given in vain;
'Tis paid with sighs a plenty
   And sold for endless rue.'
And I am two-and-twenty,
   And oh, 'tis true, 'tis true.

There pass the careless people
That call their souls their own:
Here by the road I loiter,
How idle and alone.

Ah, past the plunge of plummet,
In seas I cannot sound,
My heart and soul and senses,
World without end, are drowned.

His folly has not fellow
Beneath the blue of day
That gives to man or woman
His heart and soul away.

There flowers no balm to sain him
From east of earth to west
That's lost for everlasting
The heart out of his breast.

Here by the labouring highway
With empty hands I stroll:
Sea-deep, till doomsday morning,
Lie lost my heart and soul.

Look not in my eyes, for fear
   They mirror true the sight I see,
And there you find your face too clear
   And love it and be lost like me.
One the long nights through must lie
   Spent in star-defeated sighs,
But why should you as well as I
   Perish? gaze not in my eyes.

A Grecian lad, as I hear tell,
   One that many loved in vain,
Looked into a forest well
   And never looked away again.
There, when the turf in springtime flowers,
   With downward eye and gazes sad,
Stands amid the glancing showers
   A jonquil, not a Grecian lad.

It nods and curtseys and recovers
  When the wind blows above,
The nettle on the graves of lovers
  That hanged themselves for love.

The nettle nods, the wind blows over,
  The man, he does not move,
The lover of the grave, the lover
  That hanged himself for love.

Twice a week the winter thorough
    Here stood I to keep the goal:
Football then was fighting sorrow
    For the young man's soul.

Now in Maytime to the wicket
    Out I march with bat and pad:
See the son of grief at cricket
    Trying to be glad.

Try I will; no harm in trying:
    Wonder 'tis how little mirth
Keeps the bones of man from lying
    On the bed of earth.

Oh, when I was in love with you,
    Then I was clean and brave,
And miles around the wonder grew
    How well did I behave.

And now the fancy passes by,
    And nothing will remain,
And miles around they'll say that I
    Am quite myself again.

## TO AN ATHLETE DYING YOUNG

The time you won your town the race
We chaired you through the market-place;
Man and boy stood cheering by,
And home we brought you shoulder-high.

To-day, the road all runners come,
Shoulder-high we bring you home,
And set you at your threshold down,
Townsman of a stiller town.

Smart lad, to slip betimes away
From fields where glory does not stay
And early though the laurel grows
It withers quicker than the rose.

Eyes the shady night has shut
Cannot see the record cut,
And silence sounds no worse than cheers
After earth has stopped the ears:

Now you will not swell the rout
Of lads that wore their honours out,
Runners whom renown outran
And the name died before the man.

So set, before its echoes fade,
The fleet foot on the sill of shade,
And hold to the low lintel up
The still-defended challenge-cup.

And round that early-laurelled head
Will flock to gaze the strengthless dead,
And find unwithered on its curls
The garland briefer than a girl's.

Oh fair enough are sky and plain,
    But I know fairer far:
Those are as beautiful again
    That in the water are;

The pools and rivers wash so clean
    The trees and clouds and air,
The like on earth was never seen,
    And oh that I were there.

These are the thoughts I often think
    As I stand gazing down
In act upon the cressy brink
    To strip and dive and drown;

But in the golden-sanded brooks
    And azure meres I spy
A silly lad that longs and looks
    And wishes he were I.

## BREDON[1] HILL

In summertime on Bredon
 The bells they sound so clear;
Round both the shires they ring them
 In steeples far and near,
 A happy noise to hear.

Here of a Sunday morning
 My love and I would lie,
And see the coloured counties,
 And hear the larks so high
 About us in the sky.

The bells would ring to call her
 In valleys miles away:
'Come all to church, good people;
 Good people, come and pray.'
 But here my love would stay.

And I would turn and answer
 Among the springing thyme,
'Oh, peal upon our wedding,
 And we will hear the chime,
 And come to church in time.'

[1]Pronounced Breedon.

But when the snows at Christmas
  On Bredon top were strown,
My love rose up so early
  And stole out unbeknown
  And went to church alone.

They tolled the one bell only,
  Groom there was none to see,
The mourners followed after,
  And so to church went she,
  And would not wait for me.

The bells they sound on Bredon,
  And still the steeples hum.
'Come all to church, good people,' –
  Oh, noisy bells, be dumb;
  I hear you, I will come.

# XXII

The street sounds to the soldiers' tread,
   And out we troop to see:
A single redcoat turns his head,
   He turns and looks at me.

My man, from sky to sky's so far,
   We never crossed before;
Such leagues apart the world's ends are,
   We're like to meet no more;

What thoughts at heart have you and I
   We cannot stop to tell;
But dead or living, drunk or dry,
   Soldier, I wish you well.

The lads in their hundreds to Ludlow come in for the fair,
  There's men from the barn and the forge and the mill and the fold,
The lads for the girls and the lads for the liquor are there,
  And there with the rest are the lads that will never be old.

There's chaps from the town and the field and the till and the cart,
  And many to count are the stalwart, and many the brave,
And many the handsome of face and the handsome of heart,
  And few that will carry their looks or their truth to the grave.

I wish one could know them, I wish there were tokens to tell
  The fortunate fellows that now you can never discern;
And then one could talk with them friendly and wish them farewell
  And watch them depart on the way that they will not return.

But now you may stare as you like and there's nothing to scan;
  And brushing your elbow unguessed-at and not to be told
They carry back bright to the coiner the mintage of man,
  The lads that will die in their glory and never be old.

Say, lad, have you things to do?
    Quick then, while your day's at prime.
Quick, and if 'tis work for two,
    Here am I, man: now's your time.

Send me now, and I shall go;
    Call me, I shall hear you call;
Use me ere they lay me low
    Where a man's no use at all;

Ere the wholesome flesh decay,
    And the willing nerve be numb,
And the lips lack breath to say,
    'No, my lad, I cannot come.'

This time of year a twelvemonth past,
  When Fred and I would meet,
We needs must jangle, till at last
  We fought and I was beat.

So then the summer fields about,
  Till rainy days began,
Rose Harland on her Sundays out
  Walked with the better man.

The better man she walks with still,
  Though now 'tis not with Fred:
A lad that lives and has his will
  Is worth a dozen dead.

Fred keeps the house all kinds of weather,
  And clay's the house he keeps;
When Rose and I walk out together
  Stock-still lies Fred and sleeps.

Along the field as we came by
A year ago, my love and I,
The aspen over stile and stone
Was talking to itself alone.
'Oh who are these that kiss and pass?
A country lover and his lass;
Two lovers looking to be wed;
And time shall put them both to bed,
But she shall lie with earth above,
And he beside another love.'

And sure enough beneath the tree
There walks another love with me,
And overhead the aspen heaves
Its rainy-sounding silver leaves;
And I spell nothing in their stir,
But now perhaps they speak to her,
And plain for her to understand
They talk about a time at hand
When I shall sleep with clover clad,
And she beside another lad.

'Is my team ploughing,
    That I was used to drive
And hear the harness jingle
    When I was man alive?'

Ay, the horses trample,
    The harness jingles now;
No change though you lie under
    The land you used to plough.

'Is football playing
    Along the river shore,
With lads to chase the leather,
    Now I stand up no more?'

Ay, the ball is flying,
    The lads play heart and soul;
The goal stands up, the keeper
    Stands up to keep the goal.

'Is my girl happy,
    That I thought hard to leave,
And has she tired of weeping
    As she lies down at eve?'

Ay, she lies down lightly,
    She lies not down to weep:
Your girl is well contented.
    Be still, my lad, and sleep.

'Is my friend hearty,
    Now I am thin and pine,
And has he found to sleep in
    A better bed than mine?'

Yes, lad, I lie easy,
    I lie as lads would choose;
I cheer a dead man's sweetheart,
    Never ask me whose.

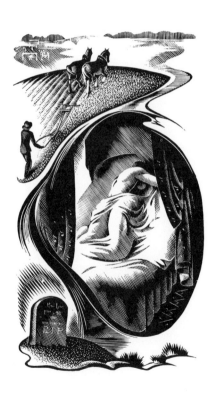

## THE WELSH MARCHES

High the vanes of Shrewsbury gleam
Islanded in Severn stream;
The bridges from the steepled crest
Cross the water east and west.

The flag of morn in conqueror's state
Enters at the English gate:
The vanquished eve, as night prevails,
Bleeds upon the road to Wales.

Ages since the vanquished bled
Round my mother's marriage-bed;
There the ravens feasted far
About the open house of war:

When Severn down to Buildwas ran
Coloured with the death of man,
Couched upon her brother's grave
The Saxon got me on the slave.

The sound of fight is silent long
That began the ancient wrong;
Long the voice of tears is still
That wept of old the endless ill.

In my heart it has not died,
The war that sleeps on Severn side;
They cease not fighting, east and west,
On the marches of my breast.

Here the truceless armies yet
Trample, rolled in blood and sweat;
They kill and kill and never die;
And I think that each is I.

None will part us, none undo
The knot that makes one flesh of two,
Sick with hatred, sick with pain,
Strangling – When shall we be slain?

When shall I be dead and rid
Of the wrong my father did?
How long, how long, till spade and hearse
Put to sleep my mother's curse?

## THE LENT LILY

'Tis spring; come out to ramble
  The hilly brakes around,
For under thorn and bramble
  About the hollow ground
  The primroses are found.

And there's the windflower chilly
  With all the winds at play,
And there's the Lenten lily
  That has not long to stay
  And dies on Easter day.

And since till girls go maying
  You find the primrose still,
And find the windflower playing
  With every wind at will,
  But not the daffodil,

Bring baskets now, and sally
  Upon the spring's array,
And bear from hill and valley
  The daffodil away
  That dies on Easter day.

## XXX

Others, I am not the first,
Have willed more mischief than they durst:
If in the breathless night I too
Shiver now, 'tis nothing new.

More than I, if truth were told,
Have stood and sweated hot and cold,
And through their reins in ice and fire
Fear contended with desire.

Agued once like me were they,
But I like them shall win my way
Lastly to the bed of mould
Where there's neither heat nor cold.

But from my grave across my brow
Plays no wind of healing now,
And fire and ice within me fight
Beneath the suffocating night.

On Wenlock Edge the wood's in trouble;
 His forest fleece the Wrekin heaves;
The gale, it plies the saplings double,
 And thick on Severn snow the leaves.

'Twould blow like this through holt and hanger
 When Uricon the city stood:
'Tis the old wind in the old anger,
 But then it threshed another wood.

Then, 'twas before my time, the Roman
 At yonder heaving hill would stare:
The blood that warms an English yeoman,
 The thoughts that hurt him, they were there.

There, like the wind through woods in riot,
 Through him the gale of life blew high;
The tree of man was never quiet:
 Then 'twas the Roman, now 'tis I.

The gale, it plies the saplings double,
 It blows so hard, 'twill soon be gone:
To-day the Roman and his trouble
 Are ashes under Uricon.

From far, from eve and morning
    And yon twelve-winded sky,
The stuff of life to knit me
    Blew hither: here am I.

Now – for a breath I tarry
    Nor yet disperse apart –
Take my hand quick and tell me,
    What have you in your heart.

Speak now, and I will answer;
    How shall I help you, say;
Ere to the wind's twelve quarters
    I take my endless way.

## XXXIII

If truth in hearts that perish
    Could move the powers on high,
I think the love I bear you
    Should make you not to die.

Sure, sure, if stedfast meaning,
    If single thought could save,
The world might end to-morrow,
    You should not see the grave.

This long and sure-set liking,
    This boundless will to please,
– Oh, you should live for ever
    If there were help in these.

But now, since all is idle,
    To this lost heart be kind,
Ere to a town you journey
    Where friends are ill to find.

## THE NEW MISTRESS

*'Oh, sick I am to see you, will you never let me be?*
*You may be good for something but you are not good for me.*
*Oh, go where you are wanted, for you are not wanted here.*
And that was all the farewell when I parted from my dear.

'I will go where I am wanted, to a lady born and bred
Who will dress me free for nothing in a uniform of red;
She will not be sick to see me if I only keep it clean:
I will go where I am wanted for a soldier of the Queen.

'I will go where I am wanted, for the sergeant does not mind;
He may be sick to see me but he treats me very kind:
He gives me beer and breakfast and a ribbon for my cap,
And I never knew a sweetheart spend her money on a chap.

'I will go where I am wanted, where there's room for one or two,
And the men are none too many for the work there is to do;
Where the standing line wears thinner and the dropping dead lie thick;
And the enemies of England they shall see me and be sick.'

# XXXV

On the idle hill of summer,
  Sleepy with the flow of streams,
Far I hear the steady drummer
  Drumming like a noise in dreams.

Far and near and low and louder
  On the roads of earth go by,
Dear to friends and food for powder,
  Soldiers marching, all to die.

East and west on fields forgotten
  Bleach the bones of comrades slain,
Lovely lads and dead and rotten;
  None that go return again.

Far the calling bugles hollo,
  High the screaming fife replies,
Gay the files of scarlet follow:
  Woman bore me, I will rise.

White in the moon the long road lies,
    The moon stands blank above;
White in the moon the long road lies
    That leads me from my love.

Still hangs the hedge without a gust,
    Still, still the shadows stay:
My feet upon the moonlit dust
    Pursue the ceaseless way.

The world is round, so travellers tell,
    And straight though reach the track,
Trudge on, trudge on, 'twill all be well,
    The way will guide one back.

But ere the circle homeward hies
    Far, far must it remove:
White in the moon the long road lies
    That leads me from my love.

As through the wild green hills of Wyre
The train ran, changing sky and shire,
And far behind, a fading crest,
Low in the forsaken west
Sank the high-reared head of Clee,
My hand lay empty on my knee.
Aching on my knee it lay:
That morning half a shire away
So many an honest fellow's fist
Had well nigh wrung it from the wrist.
Hand, said I, since now we part
From fields and men we know by heart,
For strangers' faces, strangers' lands, –
Hand, you have held true fellows' hands.
Be clean then; rot before you do
A thing they'd not believe of you.
You and I must keep from shame
In London streets the Shropshire name;
On banks of Thames they must not say
Severn breeds worse men than they;
And friends abroad must bear in mind
Friends at home they leave behind.
Oh, I shall be stiff and cold
When I forget you, hearts of gold;
The land where I shall mind you not
Is the land where all's forgot.
And if my foot returns no more
To Teme nor Corve nor Severn shore,
Luck, my lads, be with you still

By falling stream and standing hill,
By chiming tower and whispering tree,
Men that made a man of me.
About your work in town and farm
Still you'll keep my head from harm,
Still you'll help me, hands that gave
A grasp to friend me to the grave.

The winds out of the west land blow,
   My friends have breathed them there;
Warm with the blood of lads I know
   Comes east the sighing air.

It fanned their temples, filled their lungs,
   Scattered their forelocks free;
My friends made words of it with tongues
   That talk no more to me.

Their voices, dying as they fly,
   Loose on the wind are sown;
The names of men blow soundless by,
   My fellows' and my own.

Oh lads, at home I heard you plain,
   But here your speech is still,
And down the sighing wind in vain
   You hollo from the hill.

The wind and I, we both were there,
   But neither long abode;
Now through the friendless world we fare
   And sigh upon the road.

'Tis time, I think, by Wenlock town
   The golden broom should blow;
The hawthorn sprinkled up and down
   Should charge the land with snow.

Spring will not wait the loiterer's time
   Who keeps so long away;
So others wear the broom and climb
   The hedgerows heaped with may.

Oh tarnish late on Wenlock Edge,
   Gold that I never see;
Lie long, high snowdrifts in the hedge
   That will not shower on me.

Into my heart an air that kills
   From yon far country blows:
What are those blue remembered hills,
   What spires, what farms are those?

That is the land of lost content,
   I see it shining plain,
The happy highways where I went
   And cannot come again.

In my own shire, if I was sad,
Homely comforters I had:
The earth, because my heart was sore,
Sorrowed for the son she bore;
And standing hills, long to remain,
Shared their short-lived comrade's pain.
And bound for the same bourn as I,
On every road I wandered by,
Trod beside me, close and dear,
The beautiful and death-struck year:
Whether in the woodland brown
I heard the beechnut rustle down,
And saw the purple crocus pale
Flower about the autumn dale;
Or littering far the fields of May
Lady-smocks a-bleaching lay,
And like a skylit water stood
The bluebells in the azured wood.

Yonder, lightening other loads,
The seasons range the country roads,
But here in London streets I ken
No such helpmates, only men;
And these are not in plight to bear,
If they would, another's care.
They have enough as 'tis: I see
In many an eye that measures me
The mortal sickness of a mind

Too unhappy to be kind.
Undone with misery, all they can
Is to hate their fellow man;
And till they drop they needs must still
Look at you and wish you ill.

## THE MERRY GUIDE

Once in the wind of morning
   I ranged the thymy wold;
The world-wide air was azure
   And all the brooks ran gold.

There through the dews beside me
   Behold a youth that trod,
With feathered cap on forehead,
   And poised a golden rod.

With mien to match the morning
   And gay delightful guise
And friendly brows and laughter
   He looked me in the eyes.

Oh whence, I asked, and whither?
   He smiled and would not say,
And looked at me and beckoned
   And laughed and led the way.

And with kind looks and laughter
   And nought to say beside
We two went on together,
   I and my happy guide.

Across the glittering pastures
   And empty upland still
And solitude of shepherds
   High in the folded hill,

With gay regards of promise
    And sure unslackened stride
And smiles and nothing spoken
    Led on my merry guide.

By blowing realms of woodland
    With sunstruck vanes afield
And cloud-led shadows sailing
    About the windy weald,

By valley-guarded granges
    And silver waters wide,
Content at heart I followed
    With my delightful guide.

And like the cloudy shadows
    Across the country blown
We two fare on for ever,
    But not we two alone.

With the great gale we journey
    That breathes from gardens thinned,
Borne in the drift of blossoms
    Whose petals throng the wind;

Buoyed on the heaven-heard whisper
    Of dancing leaflets whirled
From all the woods that autumn
    Bereaves in all the world.

And midst the fluttering legion
    Of all that ever died
I follow, and before us
    Goes the delightful guide,

With lips that brim with laughter
    But never once respond,
And feet that fly on feathers,
    And serpent-circled wand.

By hanging woods and hamlets
    That gaze through orchards down
On many a windmill turning
    And far-discovered town,

## THE IMMORTAL PART

When I meet the morning beam
Or lay me down at night to dream,
I hear my bones within me say,
'Another night, another day.

'When shall this slough of sense be cast,
This dust of thoughts be laid at last,
The man of flesh and soul be slain
And the man of bone remain?

'This tongue that talks, these lungs that shout,
These thews that hustle us about,
This brain that fills the skull with schemes,
And its humming hive of dreams, –

'These to-day are proud in power
And lord it in their little hour:
The immortal bones obey control
Of dying flesh and dying soul.

''Tis long till eve and morn are gone:
Slow the endless night comes on,
And late to fulness grows the birth
That shall last as long as earth.

'Wanderers eastward, wanderers west,
Know you why you cannot rest?
'Tis that every mother's son
Travails with a skeleton.

'Lie down in the bed of dust;
Bear the fruit that bear you must;
Bring the eternal seed to light,
And morn is all the same as night.

'Rest you so from trouble sore,
Fear the heat o' the sun no more,
Nor the snowing winter wild,
Now you labour not with child.

'Empty vessel, garment cast,
We that wore you long shall last.
– Another night, another day.'
So my bones within me say.

Therefore they shall do my will
To-day while I am master still,
And flesh and soul, now both are strong,
Shall hale the sullen slaves along,

Before this fire of sense decay,
This smoke of thought blow clean away,
And leave with ancient night alone
The stedfast and enduring bone.

Shot? so quick, so clean an ending?
  Oh that was right, lad, that was brave:
Yours was not an ill for mending,
  'Twas best to take it to the grave.

Oh you had forethought, you could reason,
  And saw your road and where it led,
And early wise and brave in season
  Put the pistol to your head.

Oh soon, and better so than later
  After long disgrace and scorn,
You shot dead the household traitor,
  The soul that should not have been born.

Right you guessed the rising morrow
  And scorned to tread the mire you must:
Dust's your wages, son of sorrow,
  But men may come to worse than dust.

Souls undone, undoing others, –
  Long time since the tale began.
You would not live to wrong your brothers:
  Oh lad, you died as fits a man.

Now to your grave shall friend and stranger
  With ruth and some with envy come:
Undishonoured, clear of danger,
  Clean of guilt, pass hence and home.

Turn safe to rest, no dreams, no waking;
  And here, man, here's the wreath I've made:
'Tis not a gift that's worth the taking,
  But wear it and it will not fade.

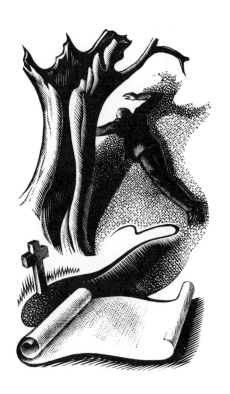

If it chance your eye offend you,
  Pluck it out, lad, and be sound:
'Twill hurt, but here are salves to friend you,
  And many a balsam grows on ground.

And if your hand or foot offend you,
  Cut it off, lad, and be whole;
But play the man, stand up and end you,
  When your sickness is your soul.

Bring, in this timeless grave to throw,
No cypress, sombre on the snow;
Snap not from the bitter yew
His leaves that live December through;
Break no rosemary, bright with rime
And sparkling to the cruel clime;
Nor plod the winter land to look
For willows in the icy brook
To cast them leafless round him: bring
No spray that ever buds in spring.

But if the Christmas field has kept
Awns the last gleaner overstept,
Or shrivelled flax, whose flower is blue
A single season, never two;
Or if one haulm whose year is o'er
Shivers on the upland frore,
– Oh, bring from hill and stream and plain
Whatever will not flower again,
To give him comfort: he and those
Shall bide eternal bedfellows
Where low upon the couch he lies
Whence he never shall arise.

## THE CARPENTER'S SON

'Here the hangman stops his cart:
Now the best of friends must part.
Fare you well, for ill fare I:
Live, lads, and I will die.

'Oh, at home had I but stayed
'Prenticed to my father's trade,
Had I stuck to plane and adze,
I had not been lost, my lads.

'Then I might have built perhaps
Gallows-trees for other chaps,
Never dangled on my own,
Had I but left ill alone.

'Now, you see, they hang me high,
And the people passing by
Stop to shake their fists and curse;
So 'tis come from ill to worse.

'Here hang I, and right and left
Two poor fellows hang for theft:
All the same's the luck we prove,
Though the midmost hangs for love.

'Comrades all, that stand and gaze,
Walk henceforth in other ways;
See my neck and save your own:
Comrades all, leave ill alone.

'Make some day a decent end,
Shrewder fellows than your friend.
Fare you well, for ill fare I:
Live, lads, and I will die.'

Be still, my soul, be still; the arms you bear are brittle,
   Earth and high heaven are fixt of old and founded strong.
Think rather, – call to thought, if now you grieve a little,
   The days when we had rest, O soul, for they were long.

Men loved unkindness then, but lightless in the quarry
   I slept and saw not; tears fell down, I did not mourn;
Sweat ran and blood sprang out and I was never sorry:
   Then it was well with me, in days ere I was born.

Now, and I muse for why and never find the reason,
   I pace the earth, and drink the air, and feel the sun.
Be still, be still, my soul; it is but for a season:
   Let us endure an hour and see injustice done.

Ay, look: high heaven and earth ail from the prime foundation;
   All thoughts to rive the heart are here, and all are vain:
Horror and scorn and hate and fear and indignation –
   Oh why did I awake? when shall I sleep again?

Think no more, lad; laugh, be jolly:
　　Why should men make haste to die?
Empty heads and tongues a-talking
Make the rough road easy walking,
And the feather pate of folly
　　Bears the falling sky.

Oh 'tis jesting, dancing, drinking
　　Spins the heavy world around.
If young hearts were not so clever,
Oh, they would be young for ever:
Think no more; 'tis only thinking
　　Lays lads underground.

*Clunton and Clunbury,*
*Clungunford and Clun,*
*Are the quietest places*
*Under the sun.*

In valleys of springs of rivers,
  By Ony and Teme and Clun,
The country for easy livers,
  The quietest under the sun,

We still had sorrows to lighten,
  One could not be always glad,
And lads knew trouble at Knighton
  When I was a Knighton lad.

By bridges that Thames runs under,
  In London, the town built ill,
'Tis sure small matter for wonder
  If sorrow is with one still.

And if as a lad grows older
  The troubles he bears are more,
He carries his griefs on a shoulder
  That handselled them long before.

Where shall one halt to deliver
  This luggage I'd lief set down?
Not Thames, not Teme is the river,
  Nor London nor Knighton the town:

'Tis a long way further than Knighton,
  A quieter place than Clun,
Where doomsday may thunder and lighten
  And little 'twill matter to one.

Loitering with a vacant eye
Along the Grecian gallery,
And brooding on my heavy ill,
I met a statue standing still.
Still in marble stone stood he,
And stedfastly he looked at me.
'Well met,' I thought the look would say,
'We both were fashioned far away;
We neither knew, when we were young,
These Londoners we live among.'

Still he stood and eyed me hard,
An earnest and a grave regard:
'What, lad, drooping with your lot?
I too would be where I am not.
I too survey that endless line
Of men whose thoughts are not as mine.
Years, ere you stood up from rest,
On my neck the collar prest;
Years, when you lay down your ill,
I shall stand and bear it still.
Courage, lad, 'tis not for long:
Stand, quit you like stone, be strong.'
So I thought his look would say;
And light on me my trouble lay,
And I stept out in flesh and bone
Manful like the man of stone.

Far in a western brookland
    That bred me long ago
The poplars stand and tremble
    By pools I used to know.

There, in the windless night-time,
    The wanderer, marvelling why,
Halts on the bridge to hearken
    How soft the poplars sigh.

He hears: no more remembered
    In fields where I was known,
Here I lie down in London
    And turn to rest alone.

There, by the starlit fences,
    The wanderer halts and hears
My soul that lingers sighing
    About the glimmering weirs.

## THE TRUE LOVER

The lad came to the door at night,
   When lovers crown their vows,
And whistled soft and out of sight
   In shadow of the boughs.

'I shall not vex you with my face
   Henceforth, my love, for aye;
So take me in your arms a space
   Before the east is grey.

'When I from hence away am past
   I shall not find a bride,
And you shall be the first and last
   I ever lay beside.'

She heard and went and knew not why;
   Her heart to his she laid;
Light was the air beneath the sky
   But dark under the shade.

'Oh do you breathe, lad, that your breast
   Seems not to rise and fall,
And here upon my bosom prest
   There beats no heart at all?'

'Oh loud, my girl, it once would knock,
   You should have felt it then;
But since for you I stopped the clock
   It never goes again.'

'Oh lad, what is it, lad, that drips
   Wet from your neck on mine?
What is it falling on my lips,
   My lad, that tastes of brine?'

'Oh like enough 'tis blood, my dear,
   For when the knife has slit
The throat across from ear to ear
   'Twill bleed because of it.'

Under the stars the air was light
   But dark below the boughs,
The still air of the speechless night,
   When lovers crown their vows.

With rue my heart is laden
  For golden friends I had,
For many a rose-lipt maiden
  And many a lightfoot lad.

By brooks too broad for leaping
  The lightfoot boys are laid;
The rose-lipt girls are sleeping
  In fields where roses fade.

Westward on the high-hilled plains
  Where for me the world began,
Still, I think, in newer veins
  Frets the changeless blood of man.

Now that other lads than I
  Strip to bathe on Severn shore,
They, no help, for all they try,
  Tread the mill I trod before.

There, when hueless is the west
  And the darkness hushes wide,
Where the lad lies down to rest
  Stands the troubled dream beside.

There, on thoughts that once were mine,
  Day looks down the eastern steep,
And the youth at morning shine
  Makes the vow he will not keep.

## THE DAY OF BATTLE

'Far I hear the bugle blow
To call me where I would not go,
And the guns begin the song,
"Soldier, fly or stay for long."

'Comrade, if to turn and fly
Made a soldier never die,
Fly I would, for who would not?
'Tis sure no pleasure to be shot.

'But since the man that runs away
Lives to die another day,
And cowards' funerals, when they come,
Are not wept so well at home,

'Therefore, though the best is bad,
Stand and do the best, my lad;
Stand and fight and see your slain,
And take the bullet in your brain.'

You smile upon your friend to-day,
  To-day his ills are over;
You hearken to the lover's say,
  And happy is the lover.

'Tis late to hearken, late to smile,
  But better late than never:
I shall have lived a little while
  Before I die for ever.

When I came last to Ludlow
    Amidst the moonlight pale,
Two friends kept step beside me,
    Two honest lads and hale.

Now Dick lies long in the churchyard,
    And Ned lies long in jail,
And I come home to Ludlow
    Amidst the moonlight pale.

## THE ISLE OF PORTLAND

The star-filled seas are smooth to-night
  From France to England strown;
Black towers above the Portland light
  The felon-quarried stone.

On yonder island, not to rise,
  Never to stir forth free,
Far from his folk a dead lad lies
  That once was friends with me.

Lie you easy, dream you light,
  And sleep you fast for aye;
And luckier may you find the night
  Than ever you found the day.

Now hollow fires burn out to black,
    And lights are guttering low:
Square your shoulders, lift your pack,
    And leave your friends and go.

Oh never fear, man, nought's to dread,
    Look not left nor right:
In all the endless road you tread
    There's nothing but the night.

## HUGHLEY STEEPLE

The vane on Hughley steeple
    Veers bright, a far-known sign,
And there lie Hughley people,
    And there lie friends of mine.
Tall in their midst the tower
    Divides the shade and sun,
And the clock strikes the hour
    And tells the time to none.

To south the headstones cluster,
    The sunny mounds lie thick;
The dead are more in muster
    At Hughley than the quick.
North, for a soon-told number,
    Chill graves the sexton delves,
And steeple-shadowed slumber
    The slayers of themselves.

To north, to south, lie parted,
    With Hughley tower above,
The kind, the single-hearted,
    The lads I used to love.
And, south or north, 'tis only
    A choice of friends one knows,
And I shall ne'er be lonely
    Asleep with these or those.

'Terence, this is stupid stuff:
You eat your victuals fast enough;
There can't be much amiss, 'tis clear,
To see the rate you drink your beer.
But oh, good Lord, the verse you make,
It gives a chap the belly-ache.
The cow, the old cow, she is dead;
It sleeps well, the horned head:
We poor lads, 'tis our turn now
To hear such tunes as killed the cow.
Pretty friendship 'tis to rhyme
Your friends to death before their time
Moping melancholy mad:
Come, pipe a tune to dance to, lad.'

Why, if 'tis dancing you would be,
There's brisker pipes than poetry.
Say, for what were hop-yards meant,
Or why was Burton built on Trent?
Oh many a peer of England brews
Livelier liquor than the Muse,
And malt does more than Milton can
To justify God's ways to man.
Ale, man, ale's the stuff to drink
For fellows whom it hurts to think:
Look into the pewter pot
To see the world as the world's not.
And faith, 'tis pleasant till 'tis past:
The mischief is that 'twill not last.

Oh I have been to Ludlow fair
And left my necktie God knows where,
And carried half way home, or near,
Pints and quarts of Ludlow beer:
Then the world seemed none so bad,
And I myself a sterling lad;
And down in lovely muck I've lain,
Happy till I woke again.
Then I saw the morning sky:
Heigho, the tale was all a lie;
The world, it was the old world yet,
I was I, my things were wet,
And nothing now remained to do
But begin the game anew.

    Therefore, since the world has still
Much good, but much less good than ill,
And while the sun and moon endure
Luck's a chance, but trouble's sure,
I'd face it as a wise man would,
And train for ill and not for good.
'Tis true, the stuff I bring for sale
Is not so brisk a brew as ale:
Out of a stem that scored the hand
I wrung it in a weary land.
But take it: if the smack is sour,
The better for the embittered hour;
It should do good to heart and head
When your soul is in my soul's stead;
And I will friend you, if I may,
In the dark and cloudy day.

There was a king reigned in the east:
There, when kings will sit to feast,
They get their fill before they think
With poisoned meat and poisoned drink.
He gathered all that springs to birth
From the many-venomed earth;
First a little, thence to more,
He sampled all her killing store;
And easy, smiling, seasoned sound,
Sate the king when healths went round.
They put arsenic in his meat
And stared aghast to watch him eat;
They poured strychnine in his cup
And shook to see him drink it up:
They shook, they stared as white's their shirt:
Them it was their poison hurt.
– I tell the tale that I heard told.
Mithridates, he died old.

I hoed and trenched and weeded,
　　And took the flowers to fair:
I brought them home unheeded;
　　The hue was not the wear.

So up and down I sow them
　　For lads like me to find,
When I shall lie below them,
　　A dead man out of mind.

Some seed the birds devour,
　　And some the season mars,
But here and there will flower
　　The solitary stars,

And fields will yearly bear them
　　As light-leaved spring comes on,
And luckless lads will wear them
　　When I am dead and gone.